STEPS *of* FAITH

FAITH M. SMITH

STEPS of FAITH

A Devotional to Catapult You on Your Path to Destiny

Suffolk, Virginia

Steps of Faith:
An Devotional to Catapult You on Your Path to Destiny

Copyright © 2020 by Faith M. Smith
All rights reserved.

All rights reserved. This book is protected by the copyright laws of the United States of America. This book may not be copied or reprinted for commercial gain or profit. The use of quotations or occasional page copying for personal or group study is permitted and encouraged. Permission will be granted upon request.

Final Step Publishing, LLC

PO Box 1441
Suffolk, VA 23439

Soft cover ISBN: 978-1-7349784-7-6
E-Book ISBN: 978-1-7349784-8-3

For Worldwide Distribution. Printed in U.S.A.

Dedication

I dedicate this book to my mother.

Acknowledgments

First, I want to give my Lord and Savior, Jesus Christ thanks for all He has done in my life. I thank Him for birthing me with a purpose and giving me a heart to love and to encourage others. If it were not for Him, this book would not have been possible.

A special thanks to my mother and stepfather, Linda and Alfred Ledee, who taught me to never give up. There were times I almost gave up and you were there for me. I thank God for a praying mother! Without my mother, I do not know where I would be. Thank you, Mama for praying me through! Thank you, Dad for the pep talks. You guys mean so much to me. I love you both.

Thank you to my sweet, loving, supportive, God-loving grandmother, Ruby "granny" Howard. Although you are with the Lord, I still owe you thanks for introducing me to Christ and teaching me how to be a lady. Thank you to my grandpa, Oscar "pawpaw" Howard for all your help and support and for stepping in as a father figure. Shout out to my Uncle Arthur Howard! I love you guys.

Thank you to my sisters: Trena Carter, Stephanie Jones, and Sheanna Smith. You guys have been so supportive! I appreciate every call, text, prayer, and words of encouragement that each of you have given me through the years. You are such amazing women! I love you, sisters. Thank you to my niece and nephews and my great nieces and nephew: Jonathan Johnson, Keondre' Carter-Monroe, Jasmine Jones, Zane, Omar, Genesis, Joshua, Jordan, and Jaylee. I love you guys!

Now to my amazing friends: Brock Harris, Shaunessy Riddick, Deneisha "Neisha" Smith, and Darius "Dae Dae" Moore. You guys have been there for me! Out of everyone who has ever crossed my path, you guys stuck around. I am so very grateful for your friendship. Thank you for allowing me to cry, vent, and figure my life out with you by my side. Thank you for the prayers, the encouragement, the laughs, and the talks. Thank you for not judging me or leaving me when I struggled with depression. I am so glad God chose you all to be my friends. I love you guys to life!

Last but not least, I thank all of my students, co-workers, and anyone who has inspired and encouraged me to be the best version of myself!

Contents

Dedication	5
Acknowledgments	6
Introduction	9
Chapter 1: Love. Maybe I'm Not Ready	11
Chapter 2: You're Almost There	19
Chapter 3: Breakthrough	27
Chapter 4: Greater is Ahead	35
Chapter 5: Beyond My Smile	43
Chapter 6: For Such a Time as This	51
Chapter 7: Do Not Fall Prey to the Enemy	59
Chapter 8: When the Promise Hasn't Manifested	67
Chapter 9: God, Can You Hear Me?	75
Chapter 10: When the Fight Gets Tough!	83
Chapter 11: No More Fear!	91

1
Introduction

Holding back tears as I shared how I felt in that very moment, my counselor asked, "Do you have thoughts of suicide?" Startled, I looked up at her and said, "No." My mouth was saying no, but my soul cried yes! "Repeat to me what you told your mother during the argument you two had during Thanksgiving," she stated. Stuttering as I repeated, "I told her, I hate that I was born because I am so unhappy." I glanced at her and then I looked out the window as I said, "I don't want to kill myself. I think I'm just stressed out with work and school." I can't believe I'm sitting in my counselor's office lying through my teeth, *AGAIN*.

Thoughts began to crowd my head as my soul cried out *HELP ME*! I knew that if I didn't get the help that I needed this time around, this might have been it for me. I was drowning deeper in my sorrows. Tears began to swell up in my eyes and my voice started to quiver. She looked me straight in the eye and said, "After evaluation, although they are subtle, you are having suicidal thoughts. You meet the criteria for major depressive disorder."

Although I was relieved to receive a diagnosis, I knew that the fight to live would continue. I wouldn't be able to do it on my own it was time for me to put my trust in God and walk this thing out in faith. When it feels like you're at the end and you can't push through any longer, will you trust God to take your hand and guide you through? This book is for every person who thought they wouldn't make it, and instead of giving up, they put their trust in the Lord. May God bless you.

1
Love, Maybe I'm Not Ready

We spend so much time rehearsing in our minds how we would like our love life to play out. We spend time considering what we will and will not tolerate in a man and what we are looking for in a man, but not enough time loving on God and trusting that in His timing He will bring love to us. We say things such as, "I want to marry the love of my life. He has to be everything I ever desired: 6'3", physically fit, educated, well-paid, faithful, honest, no children, never married, awesome home, gorgeous vehicle, pearly white teeth, loving and kind, but most of all he's God-fearing." Every time a man crosses our paths, we wonder if he is the one.

I was convinced that I was waiting to find the love of my life; he was NOT waiting on me because I was *ready*. I would say, "He is taking too long to get it right." So what did I do? I found myself jumping from one relationship to the next, and each time I thought he was the one, only to find myself single and lonely time and time again. I was the true definition of a bag lady. I held onto all the baggage of each failed relationship. I was desperate for love and I began to attract guys who were just like me . . . broken and desperate. Thoughts of *maybe my standards are too high* and *maybe I am not smart enough for the guy who has his life* together flooded my mind. It was not until a minister called me out on this that my eyes were opened. The statements I entertained in my head showed I didn't believe that I was worthy of God's love, and I didn't think that I was worthy of true love.

After taking some time to reevaluate my life, I took a step back and admitted to myself that I wasn't ready for love. How could I be ready yet continue to live life in brokenness? How could I be and I have not worked through my "daddy" issues? I share my story to say this: you are worthy! WE are worthy! God loves us and He only creates the best of His sons for His daughters. We are royalty, so why are we not living our lives as such? We must learn to love and value ourselves before any man can love us. How we think of ourselves is how men will treat us.

We must take a good look at ourselves and go to God in prayer seeking answers for how to prepare for our God-ordained mate. It may take us working through issues with our fathers. It may be healing from layers of rejection and disappointment caused by people in our lives. It could be letting go of bitterness. Many of us have a history of childhood trauma that carried over into adulthood and now it affects our relationships with family, friends, and possibly mates. Whatever the issue may be, God will reveal it to us, but we have to allow Him to heal us completely so that when the day comes for us to meet the love of our lives, we will be ready. Some experiences may require that you seek help from a professional and that's okay.

When we know our worth, we know what we deserve. The men that we thought we wanted may no longer be appealing, but now that we know our worth, we will recognize the one that comes from God. So, what if he is not as tall as you would like! He is faithful, sis! Who cares if he is not making six figures? He loves you. There is no need for us to go searching and dating every man we meet. For the Bible states, "He who finds a wife finds a good thing, and obtains favor from the LORD" (Proverbs 18:22 NKJV). He will find us, but are we in position to be found? This reminds me of the biblical story of Ruth. Ruth was in the position to be found by Boaz. The Bible doesn't state that she was dating random guys to fill the time until she found a husband. Sit back, relax, and trust that God will send your husband to you just as He did for Ruth, and you will surely be blessed.

Lord, show us those places within us that need to be healed. Let us lean on You and allow Your love to fill every void. Help us to forgive ourselves for choices we have made that were not in Your will. Help us forgive the people who have hurt us. Heal every soul wound and make us whole. May we be prepared to be the helpmates to the husbands that you have created for us. In Jesus' name. Amen.

My Journal
How have I shown God that I trust Him?

Write a Prayer to God.

What is God telling you?

Write a scripture that reminds you to trust in God's will for your life.

Complete the sentence with a positive declaration.

I am...

2
You're Almost There

"Let your eyes look straight ahead, and your eyelids look right before you. Ponder the path of your feet, and let all your ways be established."
Proverbs 4:25-26 NKJV

Fitness is a major struggle for me. There are weeks that I do well and go full force, then there are weeks that I don't want to even see the gym and I eat whatever is pleasing to my taste buds. One day I decided to take my workout outdoors. As I was jogging around the lake, I set a goal to jog a mile without stopping (I'm new to jogging), then if I felt tired, I would speed walk the rest of the trail.

As I began to jog, there were so many distractions—my thoughts, other walkers/joggers on the trail, bike riders, dogs wanting to stop and sniff me, water puddles and rocks, and the beauty of nature. It is a given that in life we will come face to face with many obstacles and situations that will cause us to lose focus. Many of these distractions will take us off our path and shipwreck our goals if we aren't careful. The obstacle could be the financial aid payment you are waiting on for classes, an argument you had with a friend, or your car breaking down the day you start a new job. Situations will arise but remember that God is far greater than any obstacle placed in your path. We can't allow these situations to deter us. Set a goal and stay the course. You are much closer than you think.

While on the trail, I had to go around people and jump out the way of bikers, but I never stopped jogging. I had my goal in mind, and although I started feeling tired and I wanted to stop, I didn't stop. Why? Because I set a goal and I was determined to accomplish it. I kept a steady pace and focused on my breathing. I know that whenever I set a goal and I work at accomplishing this goal daily, God will provide me with the strength I need. I may have to pause and reevaluate then go at it again, but I get back at it.

Don't give up, don't allow doubt to seep in. You got this! "And let us not grow weary while doing good, for in due season we shall reap if we do not lose heart" (Galatians 6:9 NKJV). I made it past the mile marker on the trail and it was only because I didn't let the distractions take me off of my path. When you feel like giving up, especially on something God has placed in your heart to do, remember that He is there cheering you on at the finish line. You may be thinking, *I will never make it*, but God is saying, "You're almost there!" The finish line is closer than you think! Push your way through. You are going to make it.

God, we thank you for giving us the strength to push our way to our destiny. We ask that You help us not to become distracted by the problems that arise, but let us keep a steady pace and achieve our goals. In Jesus' name. Amen.

My Journal
How have I shown God that I trust Him?

Write a Prayer to God.

What is God telling you?

> Write a scripture that makes you feel worthy of all God has promised you.

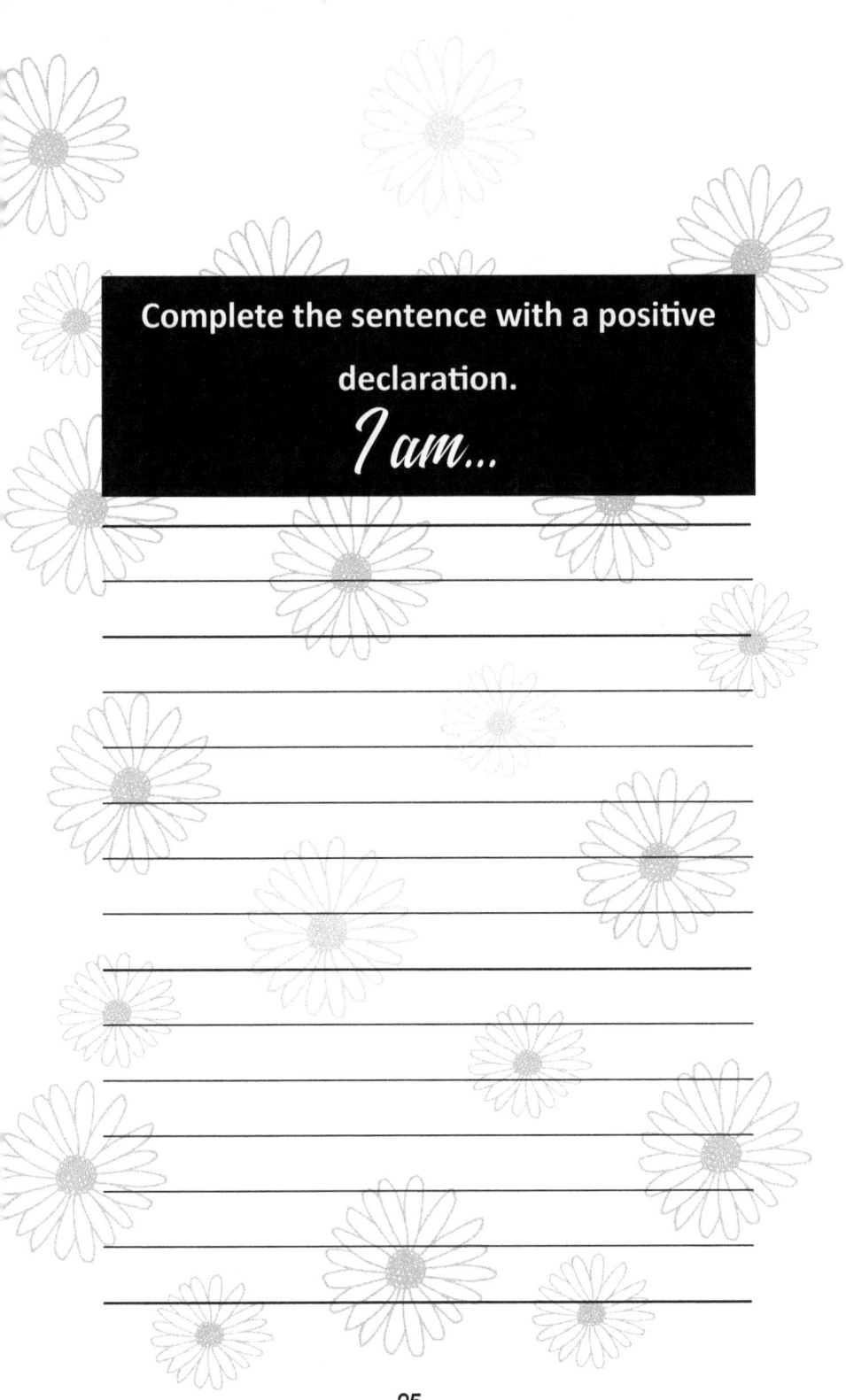

3
Breakthrough

As I scroll through social media, I always seem to come across a post that I feel is speaking to me when I need it the most. And what do they tell us to do? Type "amen" if this is speaking to you. Social media influencers are preaching sermons of hope and tossing the term around like it is falling from heaven like rain. Unfortunately, we have been trained to believe that if we type "amen" under a post on a social media, somehow or some way, breakthrough will magically appear. It has been used as a business tactic and another way to gain likes and monopolize off of believers. If I got paid for every "amen" I typed under a post, I would be wealthy. I had to remember that God doesn't work this way. He's not a popcorn, say amen, and be blessed type of God. Breakthrough takes more than a couple of comments and quoting a few scriptures; it takes work.

Several examples of breakthrough are shown in scripture. Some of the well-known stories include the following: I think about Job being tried and tested, never giving up on God and was blessed with double for his troubles. I think about the woman with the issue of blood, who believed with all her heart that if she made it to Jesus she would be healed (Luke 8:43-48). Breakthrough to me is, the woman that was bent over for 18 years being instantly healed when Jesus said, come to me (Luke 13:10-17). I also think about the lame man at the pool of Bethesda (John 5:1-18) who missed his opportunity to receive his healing because he couldn't get to the pool when the water was stirred. All of these people received a breakthrough. The catch is each of these individuals had to put in the work to receive their breakthrough. Job lost everything he had but he kept on living in faith, the woman with the issue of blood had to go into the crowd and reach for the hem of Jesus' garment, the bent over woman had to walk to Jesus, and the man at Bethesda had to "take up his bed and walk." Not only did it take doing some work, but it took faith!

When asking God for a breakthrough, we must go to the Father in faith and be prepared to do the work. Matthew 7:7-6 (NJKV) says, "Ask, and it will be given to you; seek, and you will find; knock, and it will be opened to you. For everyone who asks receives, and he who seeks finds, and to him who knocks it will be opened." Even this scripture includes action steps to our breakthrough: ask, seek, and knock. You may say typing amen under some post is an action, but do you really have the faith that God will move on your behalf, or is it that the person telling you to say amen is a really good minister and you're doing it in hopes that he or she will see it and "like" it, or is it simply out of doing what's popular? I, too, became caught up in the hope sermons (not that there is anything wrong with them) and commenting and tagging right along with everyone else. When I noticed the stagnation year after year, I had to go back and reevaluate where I was placing my faith. Saying amen isn't going to manifest my heart's desires. Thankfully, we serve a forgiving God. Breakthrough comes through Him and Him only. Let's put in the work and activate our faith so that we can watch God move!

Father God, we come thanking You for all that You have done for us. We pray that You will increase our wisdom and knowledge to know when You are speaking to us. Let us hear You clearly as we spend time with You. We ask that You activate our faith and let us not be afraid to take action. In Jesus' name. Amen.

My Journal
How have I taken action?

Write a Prayer to God.

What is God telling you?

Write a scripture that shows an example of breakthrough.

Complete the sentence with a positive declaration.

I am...

4

Greater is Ahead

"It is not possible to go forward while looking back."
—Ludwig Mies van der Rohe

Have you ever attempted to drive forward while looking in the rearview mirror at the drivers behind you, as if your stares will prevent them from hitting you? This technique doesn't go over well. Either you will crash into the vehicles in front of you or you will drive into another lane and possibly crash. So, if you know looking behind you the entire time you are driving doesn't work, why do you continue to look at your past while trying to live in the present and work towards a better future? If you are like me, you probably don't have an answer for that question. We've all done it, but we have to let go of what was and begin to position ourselves for greater.

One way to position ourselves for the blessings of God is to let go of our past. "Brethren, I do not count myself to have apprehended; but one thing I do, forgetting those things which are behind and reaching forward to those things which are ahead, I press toward the goal for the prize of the upward call of God in Christ Jesus." (Philippians 3:13-14 NKJV) Fix your eyes on what is ahead. Let go of what could have been or should have been. That relationship that didn't work out could actually be a blessing in disguise. God can't bless you with the person of your dreams if you are still holding on to that ex whom was disrespectful and unfaithful. You may not understand everything that happened in your past right now, but give it time, keep pressing, focus on your destiny, and God will reveal His plan to you. If only we could see what God has in store for us.

The moment I said goodbye to my past, God began to move in my life. I never thought I would make it, but God showed me otherwise. I couldn't progress and stay stagnant at the same time. When we continue to look back, we have to ask ourselves if we are truly ready to move forward. For those of us who say, I take two steps forward and ten steps back, I guarantee, it's because somewhere in our moving forward, we looked back. Are you willing to stop looking back and trust that God has greater for you ahead? Take that leap of faith! God is there to catch you, and because you are willing to let go of the old, He will bless you with greater. Don't be controlled by fear. Get in position for GREATER IS AHEAD!

Lord, we thank You for bringing us through the things that could have broken us. Help us to leave the past in the past and focus on what is ahead. Show us how to progress and walk in Your will for our lives. With You there is no wrong and all things are made perfect. Thank You for your guidance. In Jesus' name. Amen.

My Journal
How have I taken the leap of faith?

Write a Prayer to God.

What is God telling you?

_____
_____
_____
_____
_____
_____
_____
_____
_____
_____
_____
_____
_____
_____
_____
_____
_____

Write a scripture that increases your faith in God.

Complete the sentence with a positive declaration.

I am...

_____
_____
_____
_____
_____
_____
_____
_____
_____
_____
_____
_____
_____
_____

5
Behind My Smile

"Blessed be the God and Father of our Lord Jesus Christ, the Father of mercies and God of all comfort, who comforts us in all our tribulation, that we may be able to comfort those who are in any trouble, with the comfort with which we ourselves are comforted by God."
2 Corinthians 1:3-4 NKJV

Someone told me that some of the biggest smiles hide the most pain, but thank God that is no longer my story. Although I hid the pain that life experiences caused in my past (failed engagement, deception, lies, abandonment, poverty, hurt from friends and family and self-destruction), I smile now because I know that trouble doesn't last always. We can't allow ourselves to get stuck in our pain. Depression causes tunnel vision; one cannot see beyond the problem or circumstance they're facing. It would be wonderful if we could get the person to understand that in most cases their depression is temporary, and that things will change.

I used to smile to hide the hurt, now I smile because I am free and I took the time to heal, but healing doesn't happen overnight. Healing is a process that may require a great amount of time and desensitization; facing your fears little by little until those fears no longer have control over you. As I was healing from brokenness, I realized that I was the person that kept my pain a reality. I kept ruminating and speaking about the hurt with friends and family. Every time something would happen, I would go back and dig up past hurt and compare the present situation with situations of my past. Why would I continue to dig up old wounds?

Remember that we are not in this thing alone. God is just waiting on you to trust Him and trust the healing process. There are several stories in the Bible where people overcame the pain of life. Take a look at Joseph who was sold into slavery by his own brothers and later made ruler of Egypt. He didn't allow what his brothers did make him become bitter. He had the chance to destroy them but instead he chose to forgive and support them. Do not place limits on God. Just because it looks one way today, doesn't mean it will look that way tomorrow.

If God could show you what is in store for you, there would be no need to keep a tight grip on pain. There is nothing wrong with acknowledging that things have happened to you that hurt you, but do not wallow in your pain forever. Leave the victim mentality behind and walk in victory! You are an overcomer. Smile because you know God loves you and He would not leave you in the situation that you are in. Smile because you know that the best days are in front of you. Holding on to your pain only causes you to remain in negativity, but healing causes you to draw positivity toward you. Let your pain be a testimony, not a death sentence. Smile! Everything will be okay. What is behind my smile? The love of God is behind my smile!

Father, we know that through You we have the victory. Help us to no longer be victims but see ourselves as victors. Thank You for coming to give us an abundant life. We place our hurt and pain at Your feet. Let Your healing wash away all emotional pain and help us to never pick the hurt back up again. In Jesus' name. Amen.

My Journal
How have I overcome hurt and pain with God?

Write a Prayer to God.

What is God telling you?

Write a scripture that brings you peace.

Complete the sentence with a positive declaration.

I am...

6
For Such a Time as This

"For if you remain completely silent at this time, relief and deliverance will arise for the Jews from another place, but you and your father's house will perish. Yet who knows whether you have come to the kingdom for such a time as this?"
Esther 4:14 NKJV

Wildfires, global warming, murder, drug and human trafficking, kidnappings, innocent people in prison, school shootings, racism...the world is in chaos. Biblical prophecies are being fulfilled and it seems as if all hope is lost. However, in the midst of turmoil, God is still in control and you still have a purpose to fulfill. God always has a plan. What may seem like the end of the world may actually be a very small piece to a big puzzle. What piece of the puzzle are you? Are you the border or the missing pieces in the middle? Missionary, prophet, evangelist, nurse, doctor, counselor, whoever God created you to be, arise and fulfill your purpose!

In Genesis 25, God told Rebekah that she would give birth to two nations and the older would serve the younger. Esau was born first and Jacob second. Isaac, the sons' father, loved Esau and attempted to bless him as he was dying. Rebekah loved Jacob and overheard what Isaac planned to do for Esau and she came up with a plan for Jacob to deceive his father and be blessed. Not only was Jacob blessed by his father, but he had also taken Esau's birthright. This is what I gather from this story looking from Jacob's perspective: no matter what it may look like or how someone may appear to be taking from you and giving to someone else, if God birthed you with a purpose it must and will be fulfilled. There is no need to deceive people or lie to get what God has already promised you.

If He told you that you will be the voice of the nation, you can guarantee that you will be that voice. If He told you that your purpose is to care for the sick, be an engineer, a doctor, or a musician, but right now you are unemployed or things are not working out, stop sulking and work towards that purpose. Everyone has a destiny. You may not even believe that you are who God says you are. Believe it! You are important in this life. No man or woman no matter their position can keep you from being who God has created you to be. Don't leave this world without answering the call placed on your life.

You have a purpose to fulfill and God has equipped you with the tools to succeed. The puzzle is not complete without you. Could it be possible that you are living during these times because of what's in you? You were created for such a time as this! May we not get distracted with the things that are taking place in this world. Let's not allow the enemy to deceive us. Keep focusing on God, for He has called you forth for such a time as this. Time is winding up. What are you going to do?

Lord show us our purpose, and may we set out to do everything You have called us to do. In Jesus' name. Amen.

My Journal
What are God's promises for my life?

Write a Prayer to God.

What is God telling you?

Write a scripture that brings you hope.

Complete the sentence with a positive declaration.

I am...

7

Do Not Fall Prey to the Enemy

"If it had not been the Lord who was on our side, "Let Israel now say— "If it had not been the Lord who was on our side, when men rose up against us, then they would have swallowed us alive, when their wrath was kindled against us; Then the waters would have overwhelmed us, the stream would have gone over our soul; Then the swollen waters would have gone over our soul." Blessed be the Lord, who has not given us as prey to their teeth. Our soul has escaped as a bird from the snare of the fowlers; The snare is broken, and we have escaped. Our help is in the name of the Lord, who made heaven and earth."
Psalm 124 NKJV

Do you feel that people attack you at the most inconvenient times? You know, when you feel the most positive about life, people want to say something to steal your shine. For instance, I could be encouraging people and really feeling confident about living out my destiny and feeling good about who I am in Christ. All of a sudden someone will come and say something about my past, or when I'm feeling confident in my singleness and waiting on God someone from my past will call me. One thing I have learned over the years is that the enemy will study you. He will learn all of your weaknesses so that he can present them at times you are most vulnerable.

In order not to fall prey to the enemy and his evil tactics, we must stay before God in prayer. Be aware of the enemy's devices. His job is to steal, kill, and destroy. What is the best way the enemy gets you to fall prey to his evil works? **Through the mind.** If you notice, when the enemy is about to attack, he works his way in through your mind. We have heard so many in ministry say this, and that is because it holds true. It can be as simple as a thought of doubt thinking that God is not hearing your prayers. As soon as doubt starts to sink in you have become prey to the enemy. He tries to get you so distracted by your depression, feelings of unworthiness, loneliness, anger, and rage so that you jeopardize what God has for you and when your blessings come you don't even notice them.

Prayer is how we communicate with God and build a closer relationship with Him. We know that He answers prayers, but are you seeking His face only when you are in dire need of something? The Bible states, "Pray without ceasing" (1 Thessalonians 5:17 NJKV). You never know when the enemy is going to strike, therefore, be on guard at all times, prayerful and in the word of God. No soldier is at ease while on the battlefield. I think at times we forget how powerful prayer really is or maybe it is the mere fact that we doubt the power of prayer, or we just don't pray. Before Nehemiah left to go rebuild the wall, he went to God in prayer and fasting. I think of prayer as a preventive measure. If you stay ready, you don't have to get ready. Don't wait until you have become prey to pray!

Father, may we desire a relationship with You and not fall prey to the enemy. In Jesus' name. Amen.

My Journal

When was the last time I spent time with God in prayer? How did I feel afterwards?

Write a Prayer to God.

What is God telling you?

> Write a scripture that you can use in your time of prayer that would bring you closer to God.

Complete the sentence with a positive declaration.

I am...

8
When the Promise Hasn't Manifested

"But she said to them, Do not call me Naomi; call me Mara, for the Almighty has dealt very bitterly with me. I went out full, and the Lord has brought me home again empty. Why do you call me Naomi, since the Lord has testified against me, and the Almighty has afflicted me?"
Ruth 1:20-21 NKJV

In an effort to escape the famine, Naomi left Bethlehem along with her husband and two sons and relocated to Moab in hopes of a better life. Unfortunately, Moab was the place Naomi suffered greatly: her husband, Elimelech died leaving her to care for her sons alone. Mahlon and Chilion remained in Moab and married Moabite women. After ten years, both Mahlon and Chilean died leaving Naomi alone once again. Naomi's circumstances made her bitter.

Just like Naomi, many of us have allowed our circumstances to make us bitter. We, too, are waiting on God's promises to manifest in our lives. One has to work daily at being bitter. It seems harder to be bitter than to be anything else. Underlying bitterness is sadness, fear, anger, and hurt. The person can't see past their circumstances or see the bigger picture. This was the issue with Naomi; she could not see that Ruth was a blessing to her and that through Ruth she would be restored. God was working in the background the entire time. However, all Naomi could see was death, famine, and disappointment. She failed to realize that God was rewriting her story and setting her up for restoration.

Society suggests that women should be married in their twenties and that all women should be mothers. As I entered my thirties single and childless, I grew bitter and I was angry at God. I was desperate for love and He wasn't hearing my prayers. I started to worship the idea of marriage and made it my idol. It was all I could think about day and night. I even began to compare my life with the lives of those around me. *I should have been married, I should be further along in my career, I should be happy* is what I would say. I literally grew more depressed each day. Then I discovered the power of "yet." I'm not married...yet. Things haven't changed...yet. I haven't finished school...yet. I haven't found the perfect job for me...yet. Our story is not over. Every promise has to be fulfilled. If God has promised you some things, its guaranteed to happen. Sarah was given a baby as promised in her old age. Hannah conceived and gave birth to Samuel. Rahab was spared during Passover. I will get married and become a mother. Whatever it is that you are waiting on, fill in the blank. "I will_____." Hand over your burdens and all your doubts to God. Allow Him to rewrite your story. I promise you it will be perfect.

Father, restore everything that has been taken from me just like you did for Naomi. We thank You that the promises You have placed on our lives will be fulfilled. Turn our hearts of stone to flesh and deliver us from bitterness. In Jesus' name. Amen.

My Journal

How have I shown God that I haven't given up?

Write a Prayer to God.

What is God telling you?

Write a scripture that shows God's restoration power.

Complete the sentence with a positive declaration.

I am...

9
God, Can You Hear Me?

"Gideon said to Him, "O my lord, if the Lord is with us, why then has all this happened to us? And where are all His miracles which our fathers told us about, saying, 'Did not the Lord bring us up from Egypt?' But now the Lord has forsaken us and delivered us into the hands of the Midianites."
Judges 6:13

How many of you have felt like Gideon? You have prayed and fasted, attended church services, and studied the Bible, but feel like God still didn't answer your prayer. You have listened to others share their testimonies, the prayers you have prayed for your friends and family have been answered, and still no answer for you. What could be the hold up? Has God forgotten you? In this scripture, we see that Gideon was afraid of the Midianites and was hiding out. What he failed to realize is that God wanted to use him to deliver Israel from the Midianites.

I believe God has been speaking to me about faith. I read a post recently that read, "Sometimes faith is brutal and requires me to cling to truth I cannot see or barely believe, as I take the next step towards building or curl up in fetal position and weep."

Whoa! That was the most honest post I had seen in a while. I was shocked that a fellow believer feels the same way I do and allowed herself to share her honest experience with faith. If you come from a very religious background like I do, it feels almost dishonorable to say life has beaten up on me and I am fighting to keep my faith. We are taught to wipe our tears, stand up tall, and have faith. Unfortunately, there will be times that you will wonder if God even hears you. That doesn't mean that you don't have faith, it means that you are human and sometimes your faith gets tested. We see in this scripture how Gideon started to doubt that Israel would be saved. He asked where are the miracles we heard about. That doesn't mean he lacked faith, it meant he needed encouragement. A little encouragement can strengthen your faith. What if this is your time for growth?

The same week I read the post, I heard a minster say, "God never intended for your faith to remain a seed." We always hear the scripture comparing faith to the mustard seed and how that is all that is required. God expects so much more from us. When you plant a seed in your garden, you expect it to grow into a beautiful flower or a piece of fruit. In order for the seed to grow into something, it requires good soil, water, and sunlight. Our faith is like the seeds in the garden—for it to grow we have to take the necessary steps. That means we take every opportunity to grow our faith by reading and studying the gospel, praying and fasting, serving in the church, and fellowshipping with other believers. It is similar to the great commission; we are tasked with presenting salvation to unbelievers. You plant the seed by sharing your faith and God will provide the water and sunlight by placing a burden upon their heart to turn their lives over to Him or through other believers sharing their testimonies.

"You cannot have faith without hope. Hopelessness can never give birth to faith." Where there's no hope, there's no faith, and no faith means no trust. If there is no trust, there is a broken relationship with Christ. It is simple as that. We can't expect God to answer our prayers when we have no faith or trust in Him. We know that no relationship will work without trust. God is nothing like our earthly mothers or fathers, spouses, or friends. He is faithful and loves us unconditionally. If He promised to answer your prayers, you can guarantee that He will answer. It may not be answered the way you think it should be, but He will answer.

Stay encouraged! God could be equipping you for the fight, just like he equipped Gideon. Keep the faith, keep on hoping, keep on believing, and keep on trusting. Your season is coming, and your blessings will manifest!

Father, equip us for the fight and restore our hope in You. Reassure us that we are not fighting for the victory, but from victory. In Jesus' name. Amen.

My Journal
How have I shown God that I have hope?

Write a Prayer to God.

What is God telling you?

Write a scripture that makes you feel hopeful.

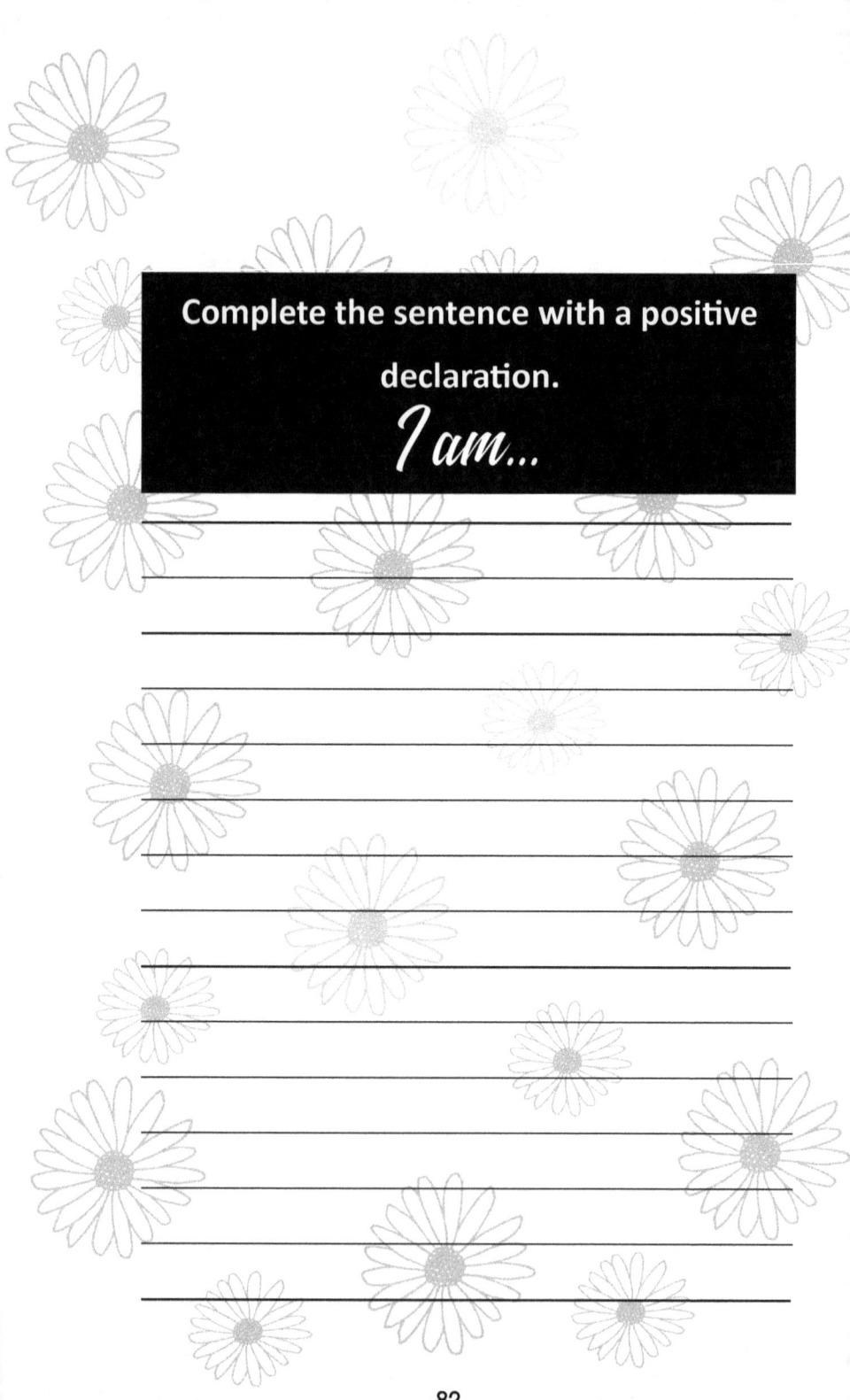

Complete the sentence with a positive declaration.

I am...

10
When the Fight Gets Tough!

"For though we walk in the flesh, we do not war according to the flesh. For the weapons of our warfare are not carnal but mighty in God for pulling down strongholds, casting down arguments and every high thing that exalts itself against the knowledge of God, bringing every thought into captivity to the obedience of Christ."
2 Corinthians 10:3-5, NKJV

Some may say it is just life, but I say it is spiritual warfare! It all started when I was recommended for a job and totally bombed the interview, missing out on a great opportunity to grow in my field. My parents were both suffering with health issues and hospitalization. It seemed like my friends had laid me on the curb and had chosen to walk away from me. I was caught in the middle of heated discussions and conflict on my job. I had published a blog only to find out it had been completely deleted. Just one thing after the other and so much at one time. Lord, please calm the storm. I am exhausted.

How many of you have felt trapped? What I am going through may not be much to some, but we all know the enemy will highlight our problems and make them appear worse than they are. The more I cry out to God, the more I feel He has turned a deaf ear to my cry for help. Some days my faith is strong, other days I lack faith all together. Some days I think I am on the right path, just to find myself at a dead end. What do we do when this happens? Will life continue on this path? Well my friends, I am here to provide you and myself with a little encouragement.

"This charge I commit to you, son Timothy, according to the prophecies previously made concerning you, that by them you may wage the good warfare." (1 Timothy 1:18) Everything that we are going through has a purpose. Sometimes this rift in life is caused by a shift ordained by God. Unfortunately, we become so consumed with the problems before us, we go into a panic and attempt to correct things and work things out ourselves. STOP! It is out of our control. We must allow God to do His work within us. What we don't see is God and His heavenly angels working behind the scenes. While God is at work, we should be waging war in the spirit and offering up thanksgiving for what is to come. Instead, we are quick to speak on the situation, complain to friends, cry like there is no tomorrow, and give up.

NO! This is exactly what the enemy wants us to do. He plays mind games, grabbing a hold to any negative thought and making it bigger and bigger. Luke 10:19 says (paraphrase), God has given US the authority to trample over scorpions and serpents and nothing by any means shall harm us. You (We) have been given the authority to speak to our situations and declare the works of God. Don't partner up with the enemy and have a pity party. God has promised you (us) too much. Why would we give up now? Scriptures like 1 Timothy 1:18 offers encouragement to keep pushing and to pray your way around obstacles because in the end you will win. There are prophecies waiting to manifest. If you give up now, you will not see what could have been.

This reminds me of a story someone told me once about a little girl and her father who were driving during a storm trying to make it to their destination. The rain beat against their windows and the father could barely see. The little girl noticed cars and trucks pulling over to the side and she said, "Dad, maybe we should pull over and allow the storm to pass." The father said, "No. I am going to keep going." The father continued to drive and eventually drove out of the storm. He told his daughter to look behind him and see all the cars and trucks that are still in the storm. He said, "If you keep driving, you will get out of the storm. If we would have stopped, we would have remained in the storm." I do not know who the author is of that short story, but if I knew, I would thank them because this story has replayed in my head for years. If we give up now, we will remain in the storm, but if we keep up the fight, we will see the light.

Lord God, remind us that when we feel trapped, You are working behind the scenes. Let us press our way through the storms of life. Thank You for giving us strength. In Jesus' name. Amen.

My Journal
How have I shown God that I haven't given up?

Write a Prayer to God.

What is God telling you?

> **Write a scripture that encourages you to continue the fight.**

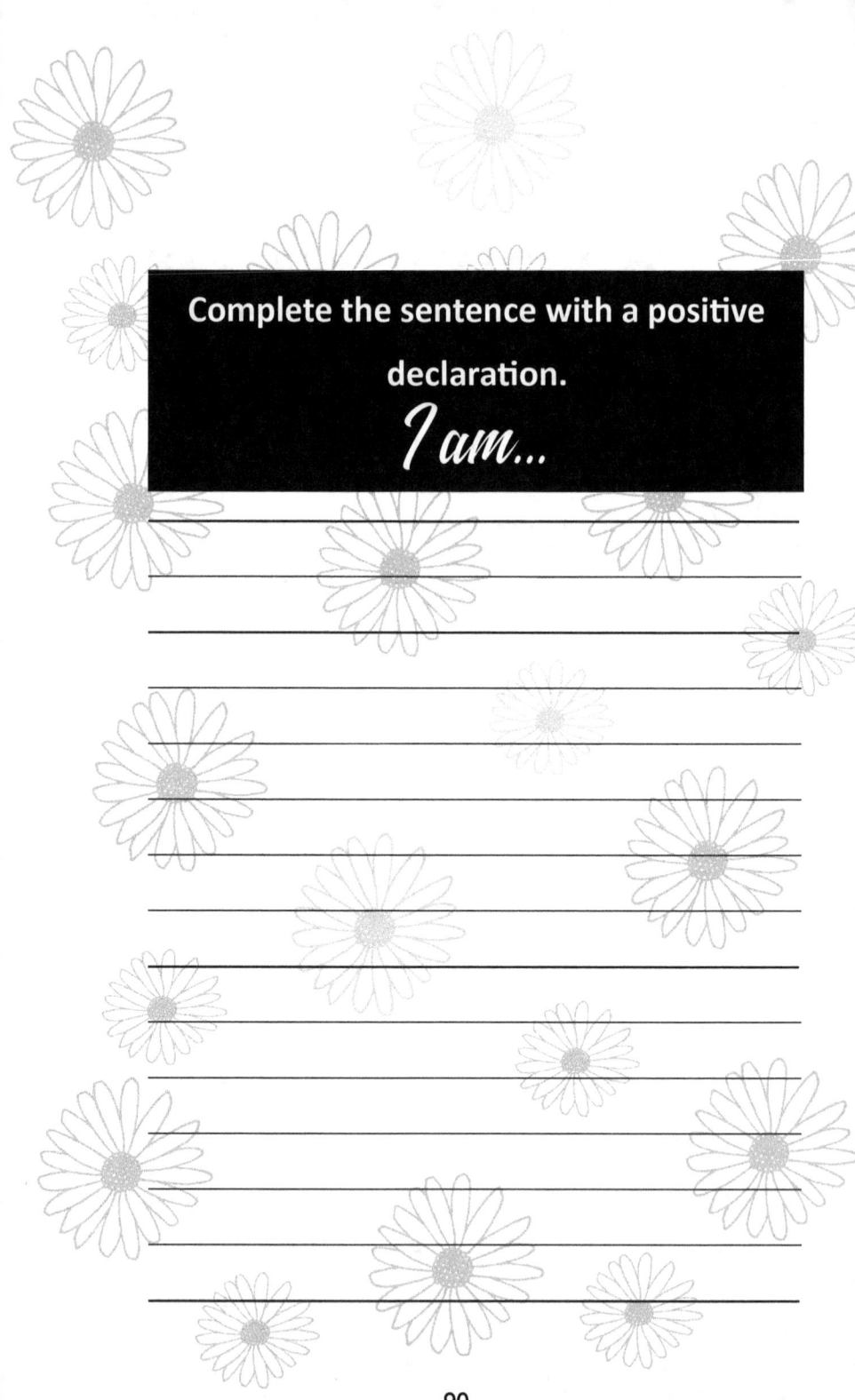

11
No More Fear!

Ding! Ding! Ding! Every hour I am bombarded with notifications on my phone and laptop. Emails with COVID-19 as the headline. Death toll and number of positive cases constantly reminding me of this virus. Every conversation turns into a conversation on virus updates, and when it's not about the virus, we are reminded about innocent black men tragically losing their lives at the hands of law enforcement.

As fear knocks at my door, I try drowning out the knocking by listening to sermons and spending time with family, but it has all become a struggle as the knocking grows louder. The more I read and the more I hear, I begin to entertain fear, anger, and sorrow. Then I'm reminded of the power of God. There is nothing greater than our God. He has never been defeated.

Why are we afraid? Is it that we don't believe God is who He says He is? Fear is like a cancer. It rapidly takes over every area of your life causing you to die spiritually. We can't feed the cancer with unhealthy food; that will only cause it to grow. We have to feed on the word of God. We must rely on the word to regain strength and to combat our fears. God didn't give us fear, He gave us power, love, and a sound mind. Take your power back. God is greater than any virus. Allow God to remove your fears. You will not be defeated.

Father God, remind us that we don't have to be afraid. Your word says that You have given us power, love, and a sound mind. Restore our power in You, our love for You, and give us a mind like Christ. Remove all fear, for with You all is well. In Jesus' name. Amen.

My Journal
What fears do I need to hand over to God?

Write a Prayer to God.

What is God telling you?

Write a scripture that combats fear.

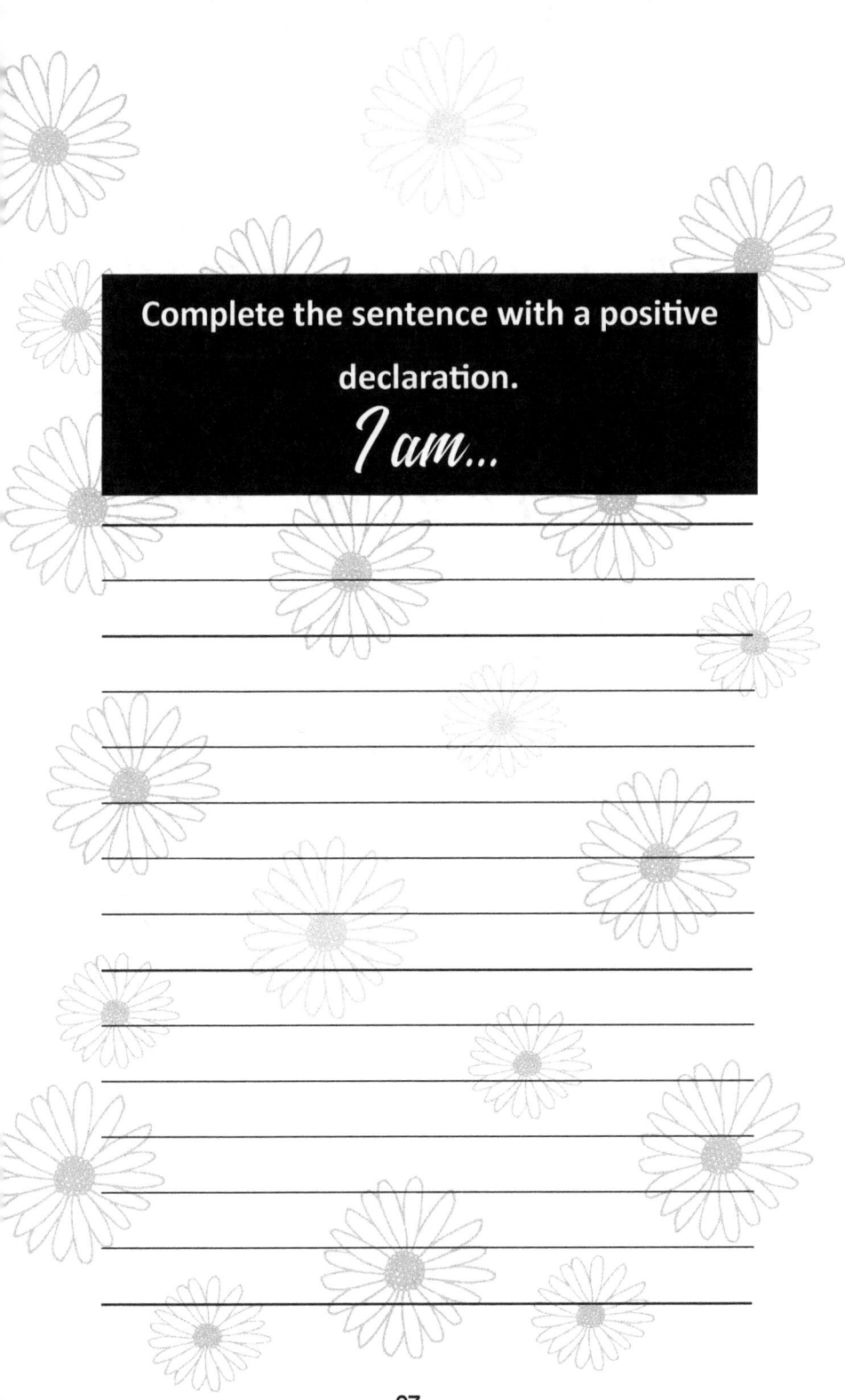

Faith it until you make it, hope for the best, and love God and yourself with every fiber of your being!

www.ingramcontent.com/pod-product-compliance
Lightning Source LLC
Chambersburg PA
CBHW071022080526
44587CB00015B/2456